What Can I Make Today?

I Can Make a
Monster

Joanna Issa

Heinemann
LIBRARY

Chicago, Illinois

Edited by Penny West
Designed by Philippa Jenkins
Picture research by Elizabeth Alexander
Originated by Capstone Global Library Ltd
Production by Victoria Fitzgerald
Printed and bound in China

18 17 16 15 14
10 9 8 7 6 5 4 3 2 1

Library of Congress Cataloging-in-Publication Data
Issa, Joanna, author.
  I can make a monster / Joanna Issa.
     pages cm.—(What can I make today?)
  Summary: "Using simple text and step-by-step instructions alongside clear, labeled photographs, this book shows how to make a monster out of an old sock and pieces of felt"—Provided by publisher.
  Includes bibliographical references and index.
  ISBN 978-1-4846-0459-5 (hb)
  1. Handicraft—Juvenile literature. 2. Monsters in art—Juvenile literature. I. Title.

TT160.I87 2015
745.5—dc23   2013039809

Acknowledgments
We would like to thank Capstone Publishers/ © Karon Dubke for permission to reproduce photographs.

Cover photograph reproduced with permission of Capstone Publishers/ © Karon Dubke.

We would like to thank Joanna Malivoire for her invaluable help in the preparation of this book.

Every effort has been made to contact copyright holders of any material reproduced in this book. Any omissions will be rectified in subsequent printings if notice is given to the publisher.

Disclaimer
All the Internet addresses (URLs) given in this book were valid at the time of going to press. However, due to the dynamic nature of the Internet, some addresses may have changed, or sites may have changed or ceased to exist since publication. While the author and publisher regret any inconvenience this may cause readers, no responsibility for any such changes can be accepted by either the author or the publisher.

Contents

Some words are shown in bold,
like this. You can find them in
the glossary on page 23.

What Do I Need to Make a Monster Puppet?

To make the body and the head of the monster, you will need **felt**, the body and head **templates**, a pen, and scissors.

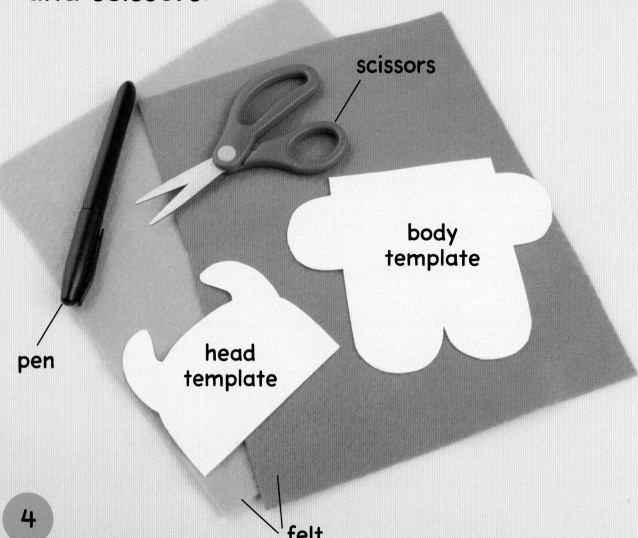

scissors

body template

head template

pen

felt

To make the templates, photocopy pages 21 and 22, and then cut out the shapes.

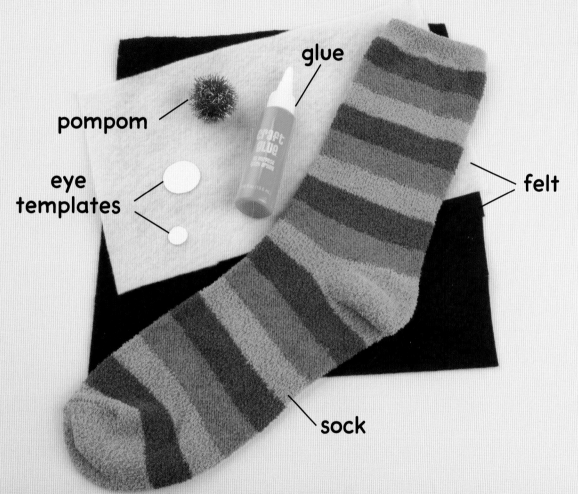

To decorate the monster, you will need the eye templates, yellow felt, black felt, glue, a **pompom**, and a child's sock.

Make the Body

Place the body **template** on the **felt** and then draw around the shape.

Cut out the body.

Make the Head

Place the head **template** on the **felt** and then draw around the shape.

8

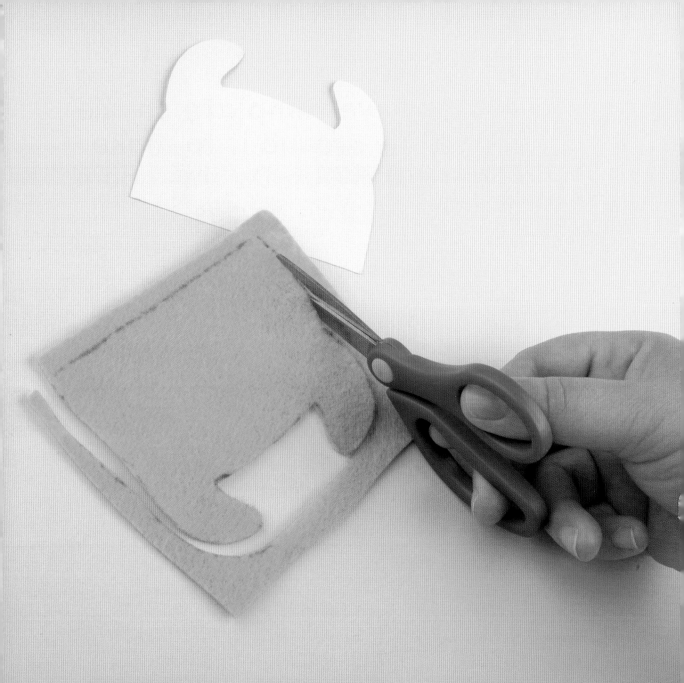

Cut out the head.

Make the Eyes

Place the large eye **template** on the yellow **felt**. Draw around it to make an eye, then cut it out. Do this again, so you have two large circles.

Place the small eye template on the black felt. Draw around it to make the middle of the eye, then cut it out. Do this again, so you have two small circles.

Make the Mouth

Cut a thin strip of black **felt** for the mouth.

Decorate the Monster

Put all the monster body parts on a table. Glue the head onto the body, then glue the eyes and the mouth onto the head.

Use a **pompom** for the nose.

Push card stock inside the sock to keep the sides from sticking together. Glue the monster onto the sock. Let the glue dry, then remove the card stock.

Now your monster is ready to play with.

Make a Different Monster

You can make different monsters. Use the **template** on page 21 to make a different head. Give your monster three eyes.

You can give your new monster **fangs**. Cut small triangles from white **felt**, then glue them onto the mouth.

Give your new monster hair. Cut a rectangle shape from **felt**, then make small strips in it to look like hair.

You can add buttons to your
new monster.

What Can You Make Today?

You could make a cute or a creepy monster for a puppet show or a Halloween party.

Monster Templates

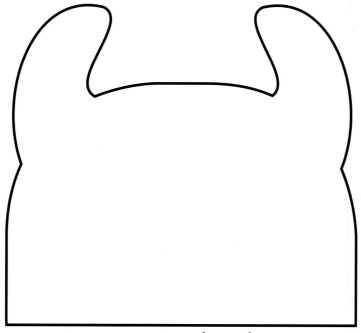

monster head

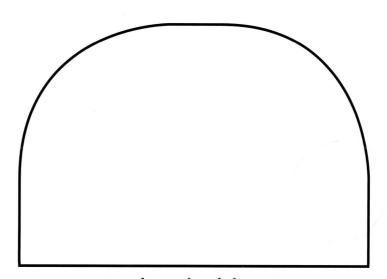

monster head without ears

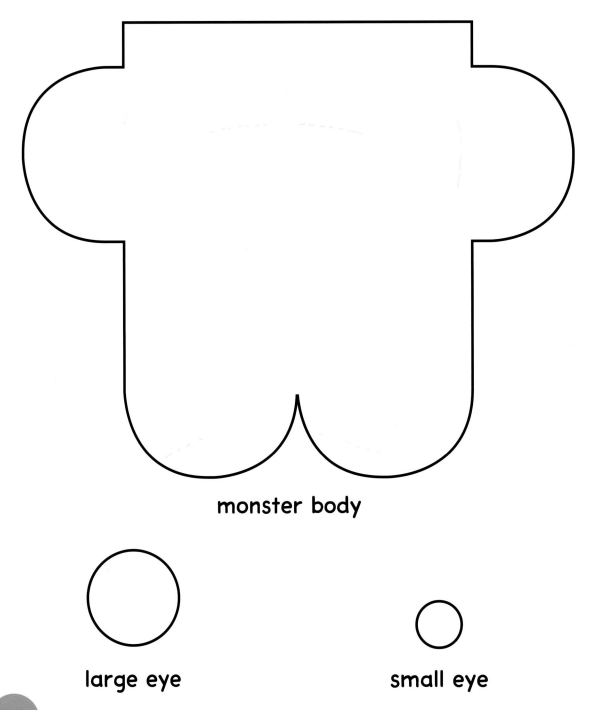

monster body

large eye

small eye

Picture Glossary

 **fangs** long pointed teeth

 **felt** type of fabric made from wool

 **pompom** round ball made from fabric

 **template** pattern of a shape cut out of paper

Find Out More

Books

Bull, Jane. *Crafty Creatures.* New York: Dorling Kindersley, 2013.

Lim, Annalees. *Fun with Fabric.* New York: Windmill Books, 2013.

Web sites

Facthound offers a safe, fun way to find Internet sites related to this book. All of the sites on Facthound have been researched by our staff.

Here's all you do:

Visit www.facthound.com

Type in this code: 9781484604595

Index